TIBERIUS CLAUDIUS MAXIMUS
THE CAVALRYMAN

Peter Connolly

Contents

Oxford University Press

Tiberius Claudius Maximus
The Cavalryman

The man who captured a king

In 1965 the tombstone of a Roman soldier was discovered in a field in northern Greece. Its unique inscription records the career of Tiberius Claudius Maximus, who served about 15 years with the Seventh Legion on the Danube at the end of the first century AD. He went on to become a cavalry officer under Trajan, the last of Rome's great conquerors.

Maximus sprang to fame when he captured the Dacian king Decebalus at the end of Trajan's Dacian wars. His exploit is shown in great detail on the huge column that Trajan set up in Rome to commemorate his victory. Unfortunately the written accounts of Trajan's campaigns, including the emperor's diary, were lost in the Dark Ages, and the name of Tiberius Claudius Maximus disappeared with them.

The great spiral sculpture that decorates Trajan's column records the main events of the emperor's wars against the Dacians who lived beyond the Danube. It draws a vivid picture of a Roman army on campaign. One can see soldiers marching, fighting and camping. The light and heavy cavalry, the archers, the slingers and the artillery are there too, all shown in great detail. But it is like watching a film with no sound track, for without the history of the period we have no idea what events are being portrayed.

Maximus' tombstone lists all the positions he held. Using this information, the sculpture from Trajan's column and the mass of archaeological evidence, the author has reconstructed Maximus' life in two books. This book tells the story of 'Tiberius Claudius Maximus the cavalryman.'

RIGHT: scene from Trajan's column showing Tiberius Claudius Maximus dashing in to prevent the Dacian king, Decebalus, from killing himself.

The soldiers' emperor

It was the spring of AD 101. The Roman frontier along the Danube was in ferment. The hastily repaired roads were crowded with troops moving into the area. Barges were being towed up the Danube, full of supplies from the Black Sea for the massive army that was assembling. Auxiliary troops kept a constant vigil from the many newly-built watchtowers and forts that lined the southern bank of the great river Danube, in case the Dacian tribes on the opposite bank launched a surprise attack. The name of Trajan was on every tongue, for news had arrived that the emperor was on his way north.

Trajan was a soldiers' emperor, having spent most of his life with the army. He had been a military tribune for many years in Syria before being given command of the legion in Spain. Finally he had been made governor of Upper (southern) Germany. He was the foremost general of his time and it was commonly believed that he would have seized power had it not been given to him.

On his way to Rome to receive the emperor's crown in AD 98–99, Trajan had spent several months in the Danube provinces. He was already planning a Dacian campaign and was concerned with the problems of provisioning a large army. The Roman forces on the middle Danube were most easily supplied from the Black Sea, but this meant navigating the precipitous Djerdap Gorge with its wooden towpath built by the legions. The towpath was frequently damaged when the river was in flood, sometimes holding up supplies for months. Trajan ordered its rebuilding, and had a canal dug to bypass the most difficult stretch of the gorge.

It was probably during this visit that Trajan transferred Maximus to the Second Pannonian Cavalry (ala II Pannoniorum) stationed at Lederata, about 15km east of the Seventh Legion's base at Viminacium. He was given the rank of duplicarius, second in command of a troop of 30 men.

Watch towers

A series of watch-towers overlooking the Danube are depicted at the bottom of Trajan's column. The towers, apparently built of stone, have a gallery at second floor level from which torch signals could be sent along the Danube at night. Smoke was used during the day. Many such watch-towers have been excavated along the Roman frontiers. They usually have a solid base with a door at first floor level. The superstructure was probably timber framed wattle and daub, plastered over and sometimes painted to look like stone work.

LEFT: scene from Trajan's column showing watch-towers along the Danube. The stack of straw was used for sending smoke signals. Most of the towers and forts along this stretch of the Danube appear to have been built shortly before Trajan's Dacian wars.

BELOW: legionaries building a watch-tower above the Danube gorge. The towpath is visible along the right side of the river.

5

Training for war

Maximus was probably only one of many junior officers from the legionary cavalry who were transferred to the auxiliary cavalry by Trajan. The second Pannonian cavalry had been posted to the Danube when the Dacian wars began.

As second in command of a troop of thirty men, Maximus probably took over their training. He must have thought back over the years to those terrible four months of his own basic training. But now the boot was on the other foot; he was going to do the shouting and beating. He must have put his men through the most torturous training, and they would have hated him just as he had hated his old centurion. He would have his men out on the parade ground riding or running from dawn till dusk. He broke them as he would a horse, and then he rebuilt them. Day after day they circled and charged the targets until they could throw their javelins accurately from every conceivable angle. He trained them to vault into the saddle fully armed, and from either side of the horse, so that they could remount quickly if they fell off in battle. By the time he had finished with them they were able to remount even when the horse was on the move.

Maximus took his troop off on long route marches into the hills, where they could practise charging up and down hill. (It is particularly difficult for a horse to charge down hill.) He forced his troopers to swim across the Danube with their horses. One cavalryman serving on the Danube claimed to have done this in full armour and then to have performed a feat worthy of Robin Hood or William Tell; he shot an arrow in the air and split it with another before it hit the ground. Even in bad weather Maximus had his men training on a wooden horse in the covered hall at the front of the headquarters. By the time that Trajan returned he had a troop worthy of comparison with the elite legionary cavalry.

BELOW: A chart showing the thirty troopers and three officers of a turma.
D duplicarius
S sesquiplicarius.
Below it, is an ala quingenaria, made up of 16 turmae, with its standard bearer (vexillarius) and commander (prefect).

Decurion

Types of cavalry unit

The Roman auxiliary cavalry was organised into three different types of unit:
1. *Ala quingenaria.* This was a 500 strong unit as the name suggests. Its actual strength was 512.
2. *Ala milliaria.* The name implies a 1,000-strong unit but it was far less than this – 768.
3. *Cohors equitata.* This was a mixed light infantry and cavalry unit, the latter making up about a quarter of the strength. The light armed north African troops used by Trajan were organised in this way. These units could be either quingenaria or milliaria.

The actual strength of a cohors quingenaria equitata was 480 infantry and 128 cavalry and a cohors milliaria equitata 800 infantry and 256 cavalry.

Ala II Pannoniorum

Maximus' unit was an ala quingenaria consisting of 16 turmae. Each turma contained 30 troops plus a decurion, who commanded it, duplicarius, second in command receiving double pay, and sesquiplicarius, who was third in command receiving pay and a half. Each turma had a standard bearer (signifer).

The ala had its own standard bearer (vexillarius), who carried a flag with the name of the ala on it. The ala was commanded by a prefect drawn from the equestrian order, Rome's wealthy upper middle class.

Prefect

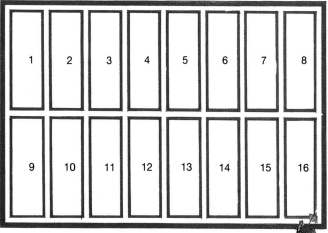

| 1 | 2 | 3 | 4 | 5 | 6 | 7 | 8 |
| 9 | 10 | 11 | 12 | 13 | 14 | 15 | 16 |

Vexillarius

A trooper practising vaulting on a wooden horse.

ABOVE: The famous cavalry signifer from Hexham near Hadrian's Wall. He is the standard bearer for a turma, and carries a signum.

BELOW: another type of signum shown on a tombstone from Germany

Training methods

Our knowledge of Roman cavalry training comes primarily from the Roman general Arrian, who wrote a manual on the subject less than twenty years after the death of Trajan.

Most training took place on the parade ground. Here the troopers learnt to mount in full armour, to gallop in close order and to use their weapons.

The parade ground was usually just outside the fort. It was levelled and the soil broken up to avoid injuring the horses. On one side was a high platform, the tribunal, from which the officers could watch. The tribunal was used as a marker, playing an important part in both training and displays.

Mounting and dismounting

The ancient writers put great emphasis on training troopers to vault into the saddle; stirrups had not yet been invented. At first this was practised on a wooden horse, the men without armour or weapons. It is not very difficult in spite of the four protruding pommels; the author has done it himself. It becomes much more difficult when it is done from oblique angles, from either side and in armour. It becomes hazardous when a real animal, which might not stand still, is substituted for the wooden horse. Arrian claims that a properly trained rider could vault into the saddle in full kit with the horse at the canter.

A Roman horseman also had to be able to dismount with spear or sword in hand. This was done by swinging one leg over the horse's withers and sliding down the side. This can cause problems as the trooper's mail shirt can catch over the pommels, leaving him swinging from the side of the horse.

Weapons training

Targets were set up on the left of the tribunal. The troopers circled the parade ground and charged, throwing one javelin as they came into the straight, a second as they drew level with the tribunal, and a third as they were veering away to the right. An exceptionally skilful rider could throw a fourth javelin back over his left shoulder.

The troopers were also taught to use their swords, learning not only to pursue the enemy, constantly striking at him, but also to lean over and strike a fallen enemy.

In the field

The cavalry regularly went on a route march. They practised alternate pursuit and retreat. In broken country they learned to jump ditches and hedges, and practised galloping up and down hill; at first this was done on soft ground to avoid injuring the horses. They also fought mock battles to practise hand to hand combat.

Trajan's army

Trajan had about 60,000 troops with him when he invaded Dacia in AD 101. About half of these were legionaries. This information is gleaned from archaeological material which tells more about Rome's auxiliary forces than the legions. The short-term presence of a legion can only be known from such things as inscriptions, tombstones, stamped roof tiles and lost equipment. Eleven legions seem to be on the Danube at this time, but few can be sited with certainty. VII Claudia at Viminacium is one of the few.

The legions

The eleven legions can be placed between Vienna and the Black Sea. I Italica and V Macedonica were on the lower Danube. Five legions, I and II Adiutrix, IIII Flavia, VII Claudia and XIII Gemina, were concentrated in the 100km between Belgrade and the Djerdap Gorge. A further four legions, X Gemina, XI Claudia, XIIII Gemina and XV Apollinaris, were encamped between Belgrade and Vienna. X Gemina and XI Claudia, posted in from Germany, may not have arrived before AD 102.

The great army sets out

A massive army has assembled in the province Upper Moesia. Five legions plus detachments from legions remaining in neighbouring Pannonia, had crowded into the area. Further down stream two more legions, the army of Lower Moesia, stood poised to launch a second invasion.

There had been a similar build up of auxiliary troops; two diplomas (see above right) show that between AD 93 and 100, the auxiliary troops in Upper Moesia had more than doubled. There were now twenty-one cohorts in the province. Similar increases had taken place in the neighbouring provinces of Pannonia and Lower Moesia. More than seventy cohorts were ready to march the moment Trajan gave the order.

Cavalry had also been flooding into the area; Maximus' Second Pannonian was only one of twenty-four regiments at Trajan's disposal. The new emperor had called in a wide variety of horsemen. They ranged from heavily armoured Sarmatians living beyond the Danube, to totally unarmoured north Africans who rode bare back and without reins, hurling light javelins at the enemy. Both types are shown on Trajan's column.

The emperor, accompanied by his Praetorian Guard, must have arrived by May. He set up his headquarters at Viminacium, which controlled the southwestern approaches to Dacia and was probably the easiest place to bridge the Danube. The legionaries had built two pontoon bridges as soon as the spring floods had subsided, so that the army could be on its way by the beginning of June when the ripening crops would provide plenty of forage.

Maximus and his troop, detached for scouting duties, would have been among the first across the river. Riding two abreast, with standards held high and helmets glistening in the early morning sun, they trooped past the emperor before setting off in search of the enemy.

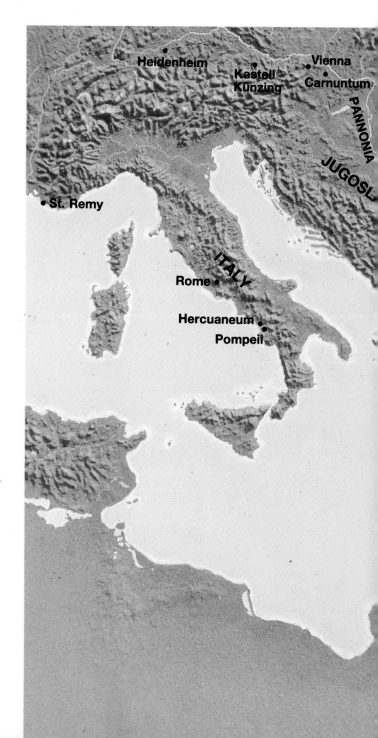

Diplomas

On completing 25 years service, an auxiliary (a non-Roman serving as a regular soldier with the Roman army) was usually given Roman citizenship. This was recorded on two small bronze plates, which were given to the discharged soldier so that he could prove his citizenship. (see p24). These 'diplomas' name the soldier's unit, and often given other units serving in the area as well as the date. Hundreds of these diplomas have been found enabling scholars to work out which auxiliary units were operating in a certain area at a certain time.

The cavalry

Twenty-four cavalry units, consisting of about 17,000 men, are known to have been in the area at this time. They included heavy-armed and light-armed horsemen, as well as mounted archers. They came from as far afield as Syria and Britain. Maximus' unit, Ala II Pannoniorum, had been in Syria. It had been posted to the Danube some ten years earlier. Trajan's column shows light-armed north African cavalry who rode without saddle or bridle, and heavily armoured Sarmatian cavalry with armour on both horse and man.

Auxiliary infantry

More than 70 auxiliary cohorts are known to have been in this area at the time of Trajan's campaigns. Over three quarters of these were 'quingenary' cohorts with a strength of about 480 men. The remainder were 'milliary' cohorts with a strength of about 800. This amounts to about 40,000 men.

Half the units were 'equitata', mixed cohorts with 25% cavalry. Nine cohorts were archers. A maximum of about 36,000 auxiliary infantry would have been at Trajan's disposal but some would have been left to hold the forts.

ABOVE: bronze trumpet with curved end from Bonn on the Rhine, Germany. This may be the type of cavalry trumpet called a lituus.

BELOW: map showing the central and eastern Roman empire where Trajan campaigned.

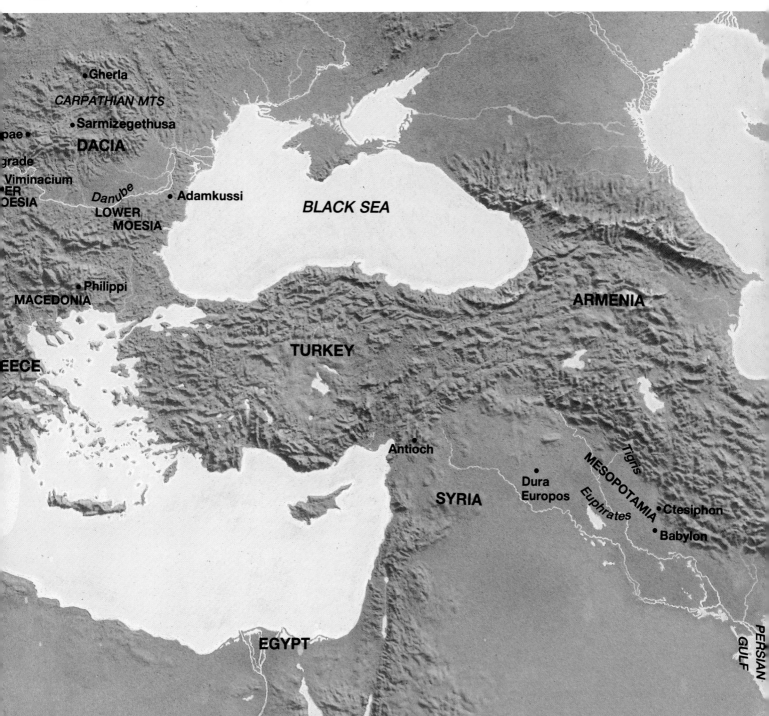

Scouting
Maximus' tombstone (see p25) says that he was a scout (explorator) in the Dacian War. It seems probable that Maximus' whole turma was detached for scouting.

A scout's duty was to make contact with the enemy and report back his movements. This required exceptional abilities. Roman scouts were chosen from the 'most loyal and intelligent men with the best trained horses.'

Return to Tapae

The great army headed northwards following the route established thirteen years earlier. The Dacians must have retreated, burning the crops, leaving nothing for the advancing army to live on. They probably withdrew along the high ground, launching attacks wherever possible.

Maximus and the other scouts rode far out ahead of the main body of Trajan's army, searching for ambushes and tracking the enemy. Often they encountered small bands of Dacians slowed down by their baggage carts and their wives and children. A few were sent back for questioning but the majority were slaughtered indiscriminately.

Once firmly in control of the lowlands, Trajan turned eastwards into the foothills of the Carpathian mountains. Decebalus retreated ahead of him until he reached Tapae, the scene of the battle twelve years earlier. He drew up his army, partly concealing them among the beech trees which grew thickly on the hillsides. Decebalus waited for the Romans to arrive.

The scouts, following close on Decebalus' heels, sent word back to Trajan. Maximus must have remembered the place well, for it was at Tapae that he had won the torques and bracelets he wore on his shoulders and wrists.

Trajan moved up with the main army and offered battle, but Decebalus refused to come down from the hillsides. The Dacian king was older and wiser now. Twelve years ago he had taken on the legions in the open and had lost. He had managed to withdraw with honour, but had left many of his best men dead or captured. This time he intended to keep his advantage. The Romans would face an attack from three sides at once if they tried to force the pass. Trajan recognized the difficulties but could hardly withdraw without trying to break through. He ordered the auxiliaries forward, holding the legions in reserve.

On the march

According to Arrian, the cavalry rode two abreast. But, in the same passage, he says that the legionaries marched four abreast. The Jewish historian, Josephus, claims that the legions marched six abreast. The width of the column must have depended on the breadth of the road. Therefore, on a wide road, the cavalry might have ridden three abreast.

It is worth noting here that Roman cavalry horses did not wear horseshoes (see p31) and, therefore, would have kept off metalled roads as much as possible.

RIGHT: scene from Trajan's column showing the Roman cavalry being sent out to battle.

BELOW: a turma of Roman cavalry attacking a group of stragglers from the Dacian army. The Dacians were probably using a 'scorched earth' policy, burning the crops as they retreated. In this case they would have taken their wives and children along with them. The cavalry would have slaughtered them all indiscriminately – an act of terrorism intended to break the morale of the enemy.

11

Heavy casualties

The auxiliaries charged up the hillsides with much whooping and shouting. Hidden by the trees, it was impossible to see which side was winning. Every now and again a Roman soldier would emerge waving a severed head to show the emperor how well they were doing. It was a bloody battle; the Roman casualties were so high that the medics ran out of dressings, and Trajan, always concerned for the welfare of his men, tore up his cloak to make bandages.

Thunder rumbled overhead as if the great god Jupiter wished to join the battle, and it began to rain heavily. The deluge must have turned the hillsides into a mudbath, and the Roman troops, fighting uphill, were forced to withdraw. Decebalus had clearly won the day. The auxiliaries had fought bravely, but Trajan knew that it was a futile waste of life trying to force his way through into the highlands of Dacia. He burned everything in the area and returned to the Danube.

Decebalus was elated by his success and during the winter he struck back. He joined forces with the Sarmatians living on the Black Sea coast, and launched an attack across the southern reaches of the Danube. It was a cavalry attack and it came like a thunder-bolt, taking the Romans totally by surprise. Trajan was probably at Viminacium when he received news of the attack. He used the Danube fleet, which operated up the river from the Black Sea, to ferry a relief force downstream. This is depicted on Trajan's column where we can see troopers loading their equipment into a barge, while their horses are being taken down stream in another.

On Trajan's column the Sarmatians are shown being driven out by the Roman cavalry, but they may well have gone before the relief force arrived. Decebalus simply wanted to show Trajan that he could hit back. If he thought that this would deter the emperor, he was wrong.

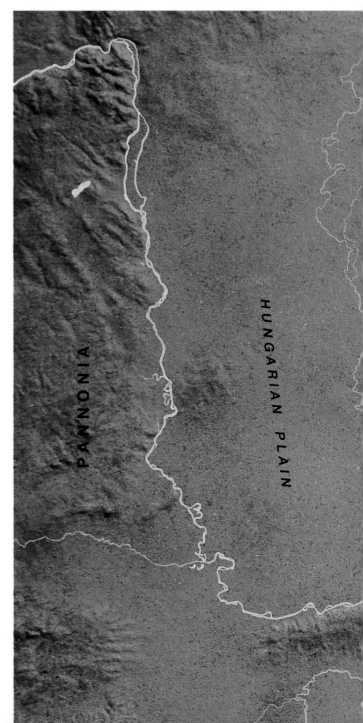

LEFT: scene from Trajan's column showing Trajan addressing his auxiliary troops.

RIGHT: scene from Trajan's column showing Trajan embarking his cavalry for the voyage down the Danube to drive out the invading Dacians.

BELOW: a model of south-western Dacia and the Hungarian plain. The Dacian kingdom extended as far west as the river Tisa.

By sheer chance a fragment from Trajan's war diary survives, as an example of Latin grammar, in a medieval text book. It tells us that Trajan advanced by way of Berzobis and Aizis.

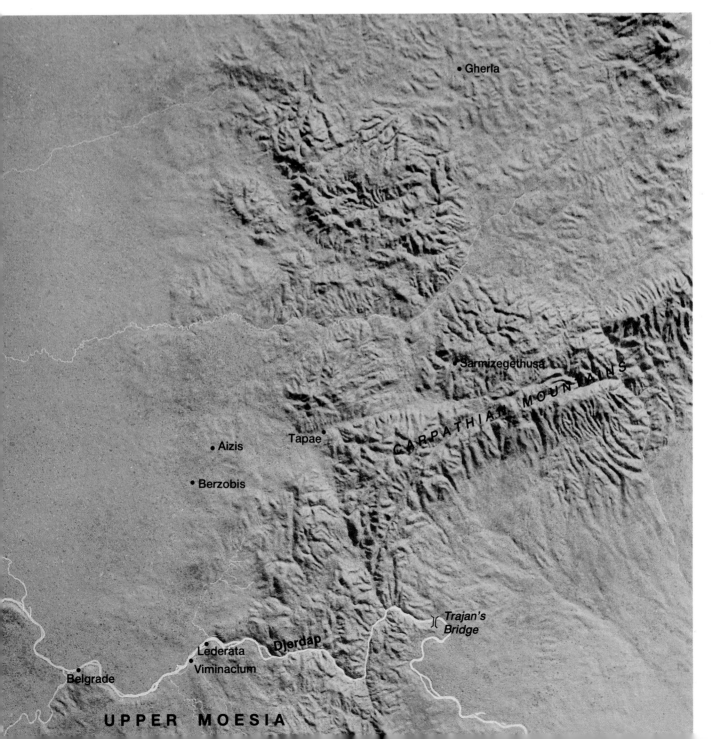

• Gherla

• Sarmizegethusa

CARPATHIAN MOUNTAINS

Tapae •

• Aizis

• Berzobis

)(Trajan's Bridge

Lederata •
Djerdap
Viminacium •

• Belgrade

UPPER MOESIA

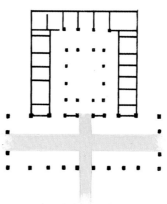

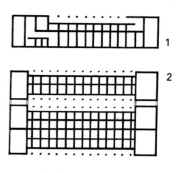

ABOVE: plan of the headquarters (principia) in the cohors equitata fort at Künzing on the upper Danube. It has a covered drill hall at the front.

ABOVE: **1**. plan of a typical double ended barracks at Oberstimm in Southern Germany. **2**. A large barracks in the ala milliaria fort at Heidenheim in Southern Germany. This is a triple barrack block probably housing six turmae.

Decebalus surrenders

The following spring Trajan crossed the Danube again. But this time he seems to have advanced on two fronts, using the two legions from Lower Moesia to launch an attack from the south-east. Decebalus was forced to split his forces and the Romans burst through into central highlands. The Dacian king was stunned. He sued for peace, but found Trajan's terms too severe and decided to fight on.

Trajan, now able to use his legions to full effect, laid siege to several of the hillforts covering the approaches to the Dacian capital, Sarmizegethusa. Decebalus remained defiant. He was confident that his hilltop fortresses were impregnable. They were certainly better built than the Celtic forts but the Dacian king, like so many others before him, failed to appreciate the overwhelming superiority of Roman siege tactics.

Decebalus' confidence remained unshaken. Even when reports began to arrive of the huge ramps of timber and rubble which were rising day by day, he refused to admit defeat. But when the siege towers were winched up and catapults started to bombard the forts, his confidence began to wane. Finally, as the hillforts fell one after another, leaving the route to Sarmizegethusa wide open, he realized that the situation was hopeless — and surrendered.

Trajan did not impose a harsh settlement. Decebalus was allowed to keep the highlands, but the Romans dismantled the hillforts and insisted on stationing a garrison at Sarmizegethusa.

The war was over and troops returned to their bases on the Danube. We don't know how many, let alone which units stayed in Dacia. Certainly the bulk of the Seventh Legion returned to Viminacium. It also seems probable that the Second Pannonian Cavalry returned to its fort at Lederata where it could guard the entrance to the Djerdap Gorge.

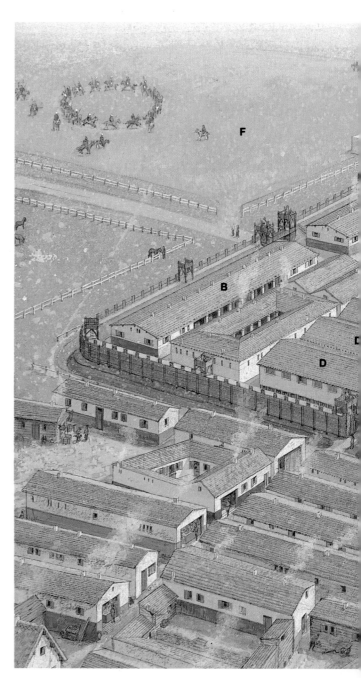

Cavalry forts

Roman forts were laid out on a cross plan, the two main streets dividing the fort into four. The headquarters was at the crossroads.

Cavalry forts followed this pattern but had some unusual features. Stables are one of these, but there are also double ended barrack blocks. These were possibly to house two turmae and therefore had to have quarters for two decurions, one at either end.

Another common feature of these forts is a covered drill hall at the front of the headquarters building, for training in bad weather.

RIGHT: scene from Trajan's column showing legionaries building a timber fort whilst a cavalryman brings in a Dacian prisoner for interrogation.

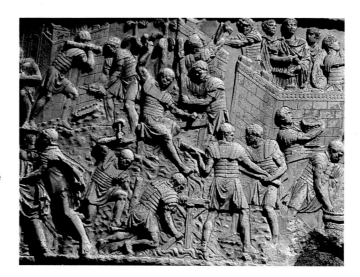

BELOW: hypothetical sketch of a timber-built cavalry fort with civil settlement in front.
A Headquarters (principia) with covered drill hall in front.
B Barrack blocks
C Commanding officer's house (praetorium)
D Granaries.
E Bath house
F Parade ground
S Stables
BS Combined stable and barracks

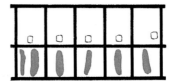

ABOVE: reconstructed plan of a stable block at Gelduba in Germany.

BELOW: pairs of barrack rooms and stables with drainage pits (orange) discovered at Dormagen in Germany.

BELOW: a reconstruction of a combined stable and barrack block discovered at Oberstimm in Germany. The cavalry were constantly training remounts to replace old, sick or wounded horses. There was never enough room in a fort to stable all the 800 or more horses used by a 500 strong cavalry unit. Most must have been left outside all the year round.

The home coming

One can well imagine the return of the Second Pannonian Cavalry after its successful campaign The troopers, their helmets flashing in the sun, would have ridden two abreast, led by the prefect and standard bearer. Each troop was led by its decurion and signifer, the latter carrying the standard of his unit. Maximus, as duplicarius, brought up the rear of his own troop.

The inhabitants of the civil settlement lined the road leading to the gates of the fort, welcoming home the conquering heroes. The women must have searched the ranks for their lovers; the children for their fathers. Marriage was forbidden, but many of the soldiers had formed permanent relationships with local women and had families by them.

The troopers lowered their spears as they approached the gates to avoid hitting the boardwalk. The sentries in the two wooden towers, flanking the gates, shouted greetings to old friends as they disappeared beneath them. The troopers rode on up the main street towards the headquarters building, glacing at the familiar plastered barracks that hemmed the street on either side. Troop by troop they formed up in front of the headquarters, protected from the weather by the huge roof that covered the street. The prefect congratulated them on their performance and dismissed them. Those with immediate duties led their horses to the stables to be rubbed down by the stable lads. The others took their mounts outside the fort and turned them loose in the paddocks. A cavalry fort would have had 4–5 square kilometres of pasture land attached to it.

It had not really been a cavalryman's war and Maximus had not been decorated; the main honours would have gone to the legionaries who besieged the hillforts and the auxiliary infantrymen for their bravery at the battle of Tapae.

Stables

Stables are difficult to identify. The long narrow buildings, without internal walls, which have been found in several Roman forts, could well be stable blocks but we don't know what they were like inside.

Similar buildings, recently excavated in Germany, are divided into small rooms with shallow pits in the floor. These seem almost certain to be stables with drainage pits.

The sizes of these stables vary from just over 3m square to 3.5 × 4m.

How many horses?

A horse must be able to get up and turn round. The Roman cavalry horse was the size of a large pony (see p.32) requiring about 2m to turn round and 3m to get up, which it does front legs first. The smaller stables could hold two horses and the larger three.

Diet

A large pony needs about 7–8kg of food a day, if kept inside. About two thirds of this is hay and the rest oats. The Romans used barley instead of oats. Put out to pasture, it needs at least 4000sq.m of good grazing and as much as 8000sq.m. of poor.

The fall of Sarmizegethusa

Peace lasted little more than two years. In AD 105 Decebalus raised the banner of revolt. He kidnapped Longinus, the commander of the Roman garrison forces in Dacia, and held him hostage. Trajan hurried back to the Danube but made no immediate move against the Dacian king. Longinus was an old friend of Trajan's, and the emperor didn't want to put his life as risk.

Believing that he had found Trajan's weakness, the Dacian king tried to wring concessions from him. The emperor played for time, discussing peace terms but making no commitments. Longinus, with selfless courage, killed himself, leaving the emperor free to act.

Trajan led his forces across the Danube the following spring, using the permanent bridge that had been constructed during his absence. This bridge, with its wooden superstructure resting on twenty massive stone piers, was one of the finest examples of Roman engineering.

This time Trajan was not waging war; he was putting down a revolt and avenging a friend. He forced his way into the central highlands along several fronts, ruthlessly crushing all opposition. The Dacian chiefs surrendered one after another, blaming Decebalus for breaking the peace. Deserted by all but his closest friends, the Dacian king retreated to Sarmizegethusa.

The Romans moved in across the densely wooded hills, bearing in on the mountain fortress from all sides. The sheer speed of the advance seems to have broken the Dacian spirit. Within days the Romans had stormed the walls and burst into the city. The desperate defenders set fire to the buildings and many committed suicide. Decebalus somehow managed to escape across the mountains with a small band of fanatical supporters. There could be no peace as long as Decebalus was at large, and Trajan ordered the cavalry to hunt him down.

LEFT: scene from Trajan's column showing the great bridge that the emperor built across the Danube following his first war against the Dacians.

Trajan's bridge

This bridge, designed by the architect Apollodorus, was built by the legions just below the Djerdap gorge. Only the abutments on the river bank are visible today. The remains of the 20 stone piers that supported the wooden superstructure are below the water. The Roman historian Cassius Dio, writing just over 100 years after Trajan's death, says that the piers were 60 feet (18m) wide and 150 feet (45m) high. The bridge did not remain in use long. Dio says that the superstructure was missing in his day and claims that Hadrian removed it.

BELOW: Trajan's Bridge over the Danube during construction.

Wanted, dead or alive

Decebalus knew that, if caught, he could expect no mercy. He fled northwards across Transylvania, aware that his only hope of sanctuary lay far to the north, beyond the bounds of Roman influence. Slowed down by his baggage train, he decided to bury his treasure in the bed of a stream. No doubt, he hoped to return one day and use the money to finance another uprising. But his hopes were stillborn. For as he fled, his friends began to desert him. One of them, trying to buy his freedom, revealed the location of the treasure to Trajan.

The cavalry spread out across the country scouring every farm and village. Their task must have seemed a hopeless one in such mountainous and densely wooded country. Maximus, with his years of experience campaigning and scouting in Dacia, was probably one of the few men capable of tracking down the fugitive king. Somehow he and his troopers picked up the trail and ran their quarry to ground.

Decebalus must have done everything he could to lose his pursuers. As long as there was the slightest glimmer of hope, he pressed on. He was determined not to be taken alive, knowing full well what fate awaited him; he would be flogged through the streets of Rome and then ceremonially strangled as part of Trajan's triumph. Finally, aware that the Roman cavalry were closing in, he climbed down from his horse and said goodbye to the few faithful servants who remained with him. When Maximus and his troopers burst through the trees, he drew his curved dagger and cut his throat.

Maximus saw the knife flash and dashed forward trying to grab the king's arm. But he was too late. He jumped down as the rest of his troop came riding up and stopped them mutilating the lifeless body. Drawing his long sword he cut off the king's head. Carefully, he tied the hair to the thongs hanging down from the front of his saddle and remounted. The head belonged to Trajan.

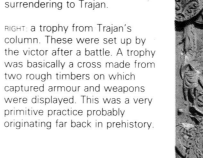

FAR LEFT: scene from Trajan's column showing the sack of Sarmizegethusa.

LEFT: scene from Trajan's column showing Dacian chiefs surrendering to Trajan.

RIGHT: a trophy from Trajan's column. These were set up by the victor after a battle. A trophy was basically a cross made from two rough timbers on which captured armour and weapons were displayed. This was a very primitive practice probably originating far back in prehistory.

BELOW: the death of Decebalus.

For bravery and devotion to duty

Maximus brought the king's head to Trajan at Ranistorum, an unidentified place somewhere in northern Dacia. The emperor called out the whole army and displayed the gory trophy before sending it on to Rome. Trajan was a generous commander. His troops were well rewarded for their loyal service. Maximus was duly honoured; Trajan decorated him and raised him to the rank of decurion. The victory would have been celebrated with parades and cavalry exhibitions. These colourful displays were a test of horsemanship and skill with weapons, performed in elaborate armour.

Trajan was determined that the Dacians would never again threaten the frontiers of the empire. He systematically set out to destroy the Dacians and their culture. Those who had supported Decebalus to the end were ruthlessly hunted down and exterminated. Thousands more were driven from their homes and forced into exile outside the empire. Fifty thousand prisoners were sent to fight in the amphitheatre at Rome. A few, the hardiest, would survive; but the vast majority would be butchered by the professional gladiators as entertainment for the Roman mob.

The fortress of Sarmizegethusa was abandoned and a new city of the same name was built in the plain to the east of Tapae. A group of retired veterans from the Danube legions were settled there. More settlers moved in from all over the empire and within a few years a new province had been created which bore no resemblance to the proud Dacian kingdom that had preceded it.

The Romans established forts throughout the new territory. A chain of these covered the route leading from Viminacium, through Tapae, on past old Sarmizegethusa and over the Transylvanian Alps. The Second Pannonian Cavalry was stationed near the end of this line, at Gherla, in the upper valley of the Samus.

The illustration shows the moment in the 'hippica gymnasia' when team **A** is attacking team **B**. As the attacker veers away, the nearest men in team **B** are allowed to throw their javelins at him.

Riders from team **B** must veer off to the left, leaving their unshielded right side open to attack. The horsemen of team **A** veer off to the right and are protected by their shields. On the other hand, a rider from team **B** can throw fewer javelins, as he must throw over his shield as he veers away to the right.

Each team had two goes as attacker and two as defender. Presumably they swapped positions to balance the disadvantages.

The weapons used in these displays do not have iron points.

LEFT: **1.** A dragon standard (draco) found at Niederbieber in Germany. These standards were used by the Dacians and are shown on Trajan's column. The cavalry adopted them for use in the 'hippica gymnasia'. They had a tail made of pieces of coloured cloth, which billowed out in wind, making a hissing sound like a snake.
2. A leather face shield for a horse (chamfron), from Newstead in Scotland.
3. Bronze eye shields for a horse, from Pompeii in Italy.

RIGHT: a partly silvered bronze 'sports' helmet from Ribchester in England. This type of face-covering helmet is described by Arrian as the type used in the 'hippica gymnasia'.

Cavalry displays

Cavalry displays (hippica gymnasia) are described by Arrian. These were a glamourized version of training exercises, performed in decorated armour.

The troopers form two teams. Team **A** is drawn up in close formation to the left of the tribunal, sheltering behind the shields. Two men form a target in front of the right end of the line.

Team **B** now rides in and charges the two-man target, hurling as many javelins as they can before veering off. The two sides then swap roles, team **B** forming the 'tortoise' to the right of the tribunal.

The Cantabrian charge

The two teams now form up in 'tortoises' on either side of the tribunal. Both teams then gallop off in close-packed single file, wheeling into two tight rotating circles, a short distance apart, in front of the tribunal. The troopers from one circling team attack their opposite number in the other team with heavy throwing spears as they approach the centre of the arena. Here again, the teams alternately attack and defend.

This is followed by displays of accuracy and rapid shooting with various weapons including slings and bows and arrows.

23

The last campaign

Maximus spent the next seven years at Gherla. He may have considered going back to his old legion as a centurion; he would not be the first to have done it, but he seems to have been happy in the cavalry. By AD 112 he had served twenty-five years and could have retired but we know from his tombstone that he volunteered to stay on as a veteran. Perhaps he had heard the rumour that Trajan was planning another campaign.

Trajan had a restless spirit and longed for action. For some time he had been looking eastwards towards the old empire of Alexander the Great. The Romans and Parthians had split Alexander's empire between them in the first century BC. There had been several wars fought over the intervening years but none was decisive. The death of the Parthian king and a border dispute gave Trajan the excuse he needed and he set out for the east.

The emperor sent for units from his old army. Among these were the Second Pannonian Cavalry and a strong detachment from the Seventh Legion. Maximus, now approaching fifty, was beginning to feel his age; his limbs were losing their suppleness and a long day in the saddle was not the pleasure it had once been.

The Parthians were squabbling over the succession to the throne and Trajan advanced unopposed. He took Armenia and struck southwards into Mesopotamia, still meeting little resistance. By the autumn of AD 114 all the northern part of the country had fallen into his hands, and he retired to Antioch in Syria for the winter. The city was crowded with dignitaries and sight-seers, coming in to get a glimpse of the emperor, when it was struck by an earthquake. The tremors continued for several days and many thousands were buried in the rubble. Although one third of the city was totally destroyed, Trajan escaped with only cuts and bruises and was able to return to the army by the spring.

LEFT: part of a diploma found in Dacia. It is particularly interesting because it grants Roman citizenship to a whole cohors equitata milliaria for their bravery in the Dacian War. The award, made by Trajan himself, is given to a cohort of Britons. The man who received this particular diploma came from Leicester (Ratae). This is an example of Trajan's generous treatment of his soldiers.

Maximus' tombstone

On the left is the lower half of the tombstone of Tiberius Claudius Maximus. It is written in abbreviated Latin. The full text would read: *Factus duplicarius a divo Troiano in ala secunda Pannoniorum, a quo et factus explorator in bello Dacico et ob virtutem bis donis donatus bello Dacico et Parthico, et ab eodem factus decurio in ala eadem, quod cepisset Decebalum et caput eius pertulisset ei Ranisstoro. Missus voluntarius honesta missione a Terentio Scauriano, consulare exercitus provinciae novae ...*

A brief translation

In short it says that Trajan made him a duplicarius in the second Pannonian cavalry regiment and then a scout (explorator). He was decorated twice in Trajan's Dacian and Parthian wars. He was promoted to decurion in the same cavalry regiment, because he captured Decebalus (cepisset Decebalum) and brought his head (caput) to Trajan at Rannistorum. He was honourably discharged by Terentius Scaurianus. Scaurianus is known to have been the Roman governor of Mesopotamia.

RIGHT: three decorated phalerae from Lauersfort in Germany. Although this type of decoration could be won by ordinary legionaries, they are often seen as part of a centurion's decorations.

ABOVE: the two sets of torques and armillae shown on Maximus' tombstone.

BELOW: Maximus being decorated for the last time. During his long career, he must have received at least one set of phalarae and possibly the gold crown (corona aurea), which he is seen receiving here. The horse's decorations are not awards for bravery but they might well have been given for skills in the 'hippica gymnasia'.

The end of the road

Trajan's invasion of southern Mesopotamia was two pronged: half the army advanced down the river Euphrates with a fleet that had been constructed during the winter, whilst the other half crossed the river Tigris and marched down its eastern bank. The two armies converged on Ctesiphon, the Parthian winter capital. Part of the fleet had to be dragged across the desert so that it could be used on the Tigris to besiege the royal city. The siege was short. Ctesiphon surrendered after only a token resistance and the rest of Mesopotamia was occupied. The emperor had gained his objective, the war came to an end and provincial governments were set up. Trajan must have felt a certain uneasiness. It had all been a little too easy.

It was the end of Maximus' career. He had served nearly thirty years. Trajan decorated him for the last time and he was given an honourable discharge. As a decurion, Maximus was entitled to more elaborate decorations than the torques and bracelets carved at the top of his tombstone. These decorations were probably shown on the base which is missing. Part of the victorious army had been disbanded and Maximus probably returned to Europe with them. He settled at the old colony of Philippi in northern Greece. Meanwhile, Trajan sailed in triumph down the Tigris to the Persian Gulf, and returned up the Euphrates to Babylon. He has scarcely arrived before the Parthians struck back in the north and the new provinces revolted. Trajan managed to put down the revolt but trouble was brewing elsewhere in the empire. His health failing, he retired to Syria where he died in August AD 117. His successor, Hadrian, withdrew the army giving up the newly conquered territories.

We know that Maximus lived on after the death of Trajan because he refers to the 'divine' Trajan on his tombstone. This was a title that was only bestowed on an emperor after his death.

Maximus' decorations

Two torques and two armillae (bracelets) are carved at the top of Maximus' tombstone. These are two of the lesser decorations and it seems unbelievable that Maximus won nothing more. He had been a cavalryman and a standard bearer in the Seventh Legion. Gaius Marius, a cavalryman in legion I Germanica was awarded a set of phalerae, large decorated discs worn on the chest. As a decurion, Maximus was nearly the equivalent of a centurion and must have been entitled to win a gold crown (corona aurea).

ABOVE: one of the saddles on the Arch of Orange in southern France. It has decorated plaques attached to the thongs that hang down from the front and back of the saddle (see p30).

Cavalry Armour and Weapons

Armour

The Roman cavalryman wore an iron helmet and a mail or scale shirt, but seldom any protection for the right arm or leg.

Helmets

Roman cavalry helmets were usually made of iron with a decorated bronze facing. Several very elaborate examples have been found in the last few years. These cover most of the head, leaving only the eyes, nose and mouth uncovered.

Cuirasses

The cuirass was made of mail or scale. It was normally short, only coming down to the hips, where it was split at the sides to allow the rider to sit astride his horse. It was double thickness on the upper back with two flaps coming forward, over the shoulders, to be held in place by a double hook on the chest.

Weapons

The Roman cavalry used a great variety of weapons. Arrian tells us that the cavalry practised with spears, javelins, darts and sling shot or stones. There were even whole regiments of horse archers.

Spears and javelins

Most tombstones show cavalrymen fighting with heavy spears, which may be throwable. Maximus' tombstone shows him with two spears or javelins. The fact he has two, means one must be throwable.

The Jewish historian Josephus, says that the Roman cavalry in Syria carried a very long spear and a quiver with three or more large javelins.

Swords

The Roman cavalry used a long sword (spatha) which they wore on the right side, suspended either from a belt or from a baldric passing over the left shoulder. The blade length of these swords varies from 0.65m to over 0.8m.

ABOVE: Tiberius Claudius Maximus as he appears on Trajan's column. He wears a short mail shirt with darts at the shoulders and hips.

ABOVE: part of a tombstone from Germany. The cut of the mail shirt is typical of the first century AD.

LEFT: part of the tombstone of Flavius Bassus, late first century AD. He wears a helmet decorated to look like hair, and a short mail shirt. Note the saddle pommels.

1. An iron cavalry helmet from Newstead, Scotland. The rivet holes show where a decorated bronze facing was fixed to it.

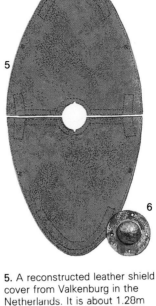

5. A reconstructed leather shield cover from Valkenburg in the Netherlands. It is about 1.28m long and 0.65m wide, covering a shield about 1.18m long and 0.55m wide.
6. Typical bronze shield boss.

Cavalry weapons: scale 1:6

10 and **11.** Two spear heads from Newstead in Scotland.
12. A spatha from Newstead in Scotland.
13. The chape from a spatha scabbard. Found at Rottweil.

14. Part of a hook fastener for holding the shoulder pieces to the chest of a mail shirt.
14a. The fastener reconstructed.
15. A Roman spur.

2. An iron cavalry helmet from Koblenz-Bubenheim, Germany. It has a bronze facing made to look like hair. The whole helmet was faced with bronze.
3. A simply decorated cavalry cheek-piece from Nijmegen, Netherlands.
4. A highly decorated cavalry cheek-piece found in the river Waal in the Netherlands.

7. Roman mail was made of alternate rows of punched or hammer-welded rings joined by rows of riveted rings.

8. Typical Roman scales. They were wired and laced together before being sewn onto a fabric undergarment: (scale 1:1).

9. Part of a scale shirt from Dura Europus in Syria. These scales were wired together and sewn directly to the fabric.

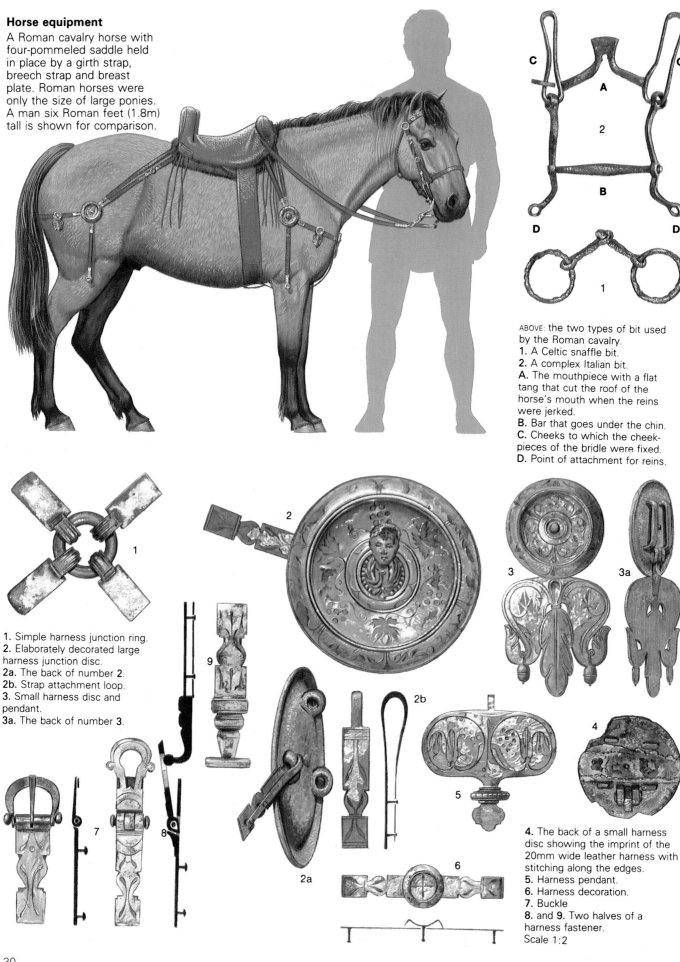

Horse equipment

A Roman cavalry horse with four-pommeled saddle held in place by a girth strap, breech strap and breast plate. Roman horses were only the size of large ponies. A man six Roman feet (1.8m) tall is shown for comparison.

ABOVE: the two types of bit used by the Roman cavalry.
1. A Celtic snaffle bit.
2. A complex Italian bit.
A. The mouthpiece with a flat tang that cut the roof of the horse's mouth when the reins were jerked.
B. Bar that goes under the chin.
C. Cheeks to which the cheek-pieces of the bridle were fixed.
D. Point of attachment for reins.

1. Simple harness junction ring.
2. Elaborately decorated large harness junction disc.
2a. The back of number 2.
2b. Strap attachment loop.
3. Small harness disc and pendant.
3a. The back of number 3.

4. The back of a small harness disc showing the imprint of the 20mm wide leather harness with stitching along the edges.
5. Harness pendant.
6. Harness decoration.
7. Buckle
8. and 9. Two halves of a harness fastener.
Scale 1:2

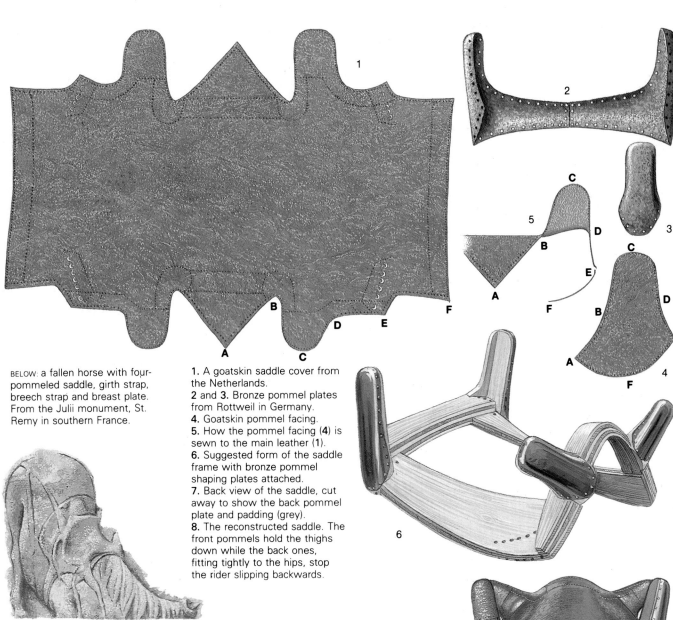

BELOW: a fallen horse with four-pommeled saddle, girth strap, breech strap and breast plate. From the Julii monument, St. Remy in southern France.

1. A goatskin saddle cover from the Netherlands.
2 and 3. Bronze pommel plates from Rottweil in Germany.
4. Goatskin pommel facing.
5. How the pommel facing (4) is sewn to the main leather (1).
6. Suggested form of the saddle frame with bronze pommel shaping plates attached.
7. Back view of the saddle, cut away to show the back pommel plate and padding (grey).
8. The reconstructed saddle. The front pommels hold the thighs down while the back ones, fitting tightly to the hips, stop the rider slipping backwards.

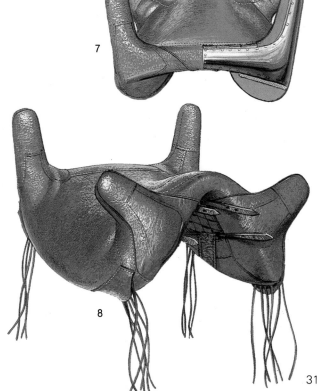

Roman cavalry horses

A few years ago the skeletons of 31 horses were found at the Roman cavalry fort at Krefeld in Germany. Most were 4–5 year-olds, averaging just over 14 hands (145cm) in height – the size of a large pony. None wore shoes. (Horse shoes have been found but not in cavalry forts.)

The saddle

Saddles are shown on many Roman monuments. These usually have four pommels. The only possible reason for the pommels is to keep the rider on the horse. Rodeo saddles have similar pommels, which keep the rider in the saddle when roping cattle. Such a saddle needs a rigid frame, otherwise the pommels cannot function.

Reconstructing the saddle

The dimensions of the frame were worked out from the leather saddle cover (above number 1). The bronze pommel plates (2) gave the exact shape of the back of the saddle. The front was determined by the shape of the horse's withers. The seat could have been made of cross webbing.

Four pieces of leather (number 4) were sewn in the main piece at B-C-D forming four 'pockets'. Having soaked the leather thoroughly, the four 'pockets' were fitted over the pommels and padded. A-B and E-F on the main leather were pulled tightly under the frame and stitched to the corresponding points on the lower part of the pommel facing (4). The leather was then left to shrink into shape.

Index

Peter Connolly is an honorary research fellow of the Institute of Archaeology, University College, London, and a fellow of the Society of Antiquaries. He is the author and illustrator of *The Roman Army, The Greek Armies, Hannibal and the Enemies of Rome, Pompeii, Greece and Rome at War, Living in the Time of Jesus of Nazareth,* and *The Legend of Odysseus* for which he won *The Times Educational Supplement* Information Book Award.

The author would like to thank the following for their advice and help: Dr Brian Dobson, Mr Mark Hassall, Dr Margaret Roxan, Professor John Mann, Dr Valerie Maxfield, Mr Michael Dobson and Mrs Patricia Druce.

Oxford University Press, Great Clarendon Street, Oxford OX2 6DP

Oxford New York Athens Auckland Bangkok Bogotá Bombay Buenos Aires Calcutta Cape Town Dar es Salaam Delhi Florence Hong Kong Istanbul Karachi Kuala Lumpur Madras Madrid Melbourne Mexico City Nairobi Paris Singapore Taipei Tokyo Toronto

and associated companies in
Berlin Ibadan

Oxford is a trade mark of Oxford University Press

© Peter Connolly 1988

First published in paperback 1997

ISBN 0-19-910424-7

Typeset by Tradespools Ltd, Frome, Somerset
Printed in Hong Kong